ZAYDO POTATO

ALLAH L♥VES ME

D1737582

by Randa Taftaf & Maz Galini

Illustrated by Lovyaa Garg

To our zany little book worm Zayd,
May your life always be blessed with the love of
Allah.
To our wonderful supportive families
(Taftaf/Ghalayini),
We love you!
To Christy, Hend, Jane, Lina, Mirna,
Thank you for all of your support!
Love,
Randa and Maz

Copyright © 2017 by Randa Taftaf and Maz Galini
Copyright © 2017 by Lovyaa Garg
Edited by Christy Williams

Published in 2017 by Rummana Publishing Inc.

All rights reserved. No part of this book may be
reproduced or transmitted in any form or by any
means, electronic or mechanical, including
photocopying, recording, or by any information
storage and retrieval system without permission in
writing from the publisher.

Rummana Publishing Inc.
PO Box 354
Riverview, FL 33568, USA
www.rummanapublishing.com
Library of Congress Control Number: 2017911840
Rummana Publishing Inc., Riverview, FL
ISBN 978-0-9990610-0-8

"When Allah loves someone he calls to Jibreel (as) saying, 'O Jibreel, I love such and such a person, so love him.' Then Jibreel will call to the (angels) of the heavens, 'Allah loves such and such a person so love him.' And the angels will love [that person]. And then Allah will place acceptance on earth for that believer."
(Bukhari and Muslim)

I know my mommy loves me...

I can see it when her eyes
shine bright..

1

I know my mommy loves me...

I can feel it when she
hugs me tight.

I know my daddy loves me...

He's my biggest fan!

I know my daddy loves me...

He calls me his `Little Man.`

I know my grandma loves me...

9

She always makes me yummy food.

I know my grandpa loves me...

11

He knows how to put me in a good mood.

I know my sister loves me...

as she always tells me so.

I know my brother loves me...

although he doesn't always show.

16

I know my aunt loves me...

because when it comes to me,
she always finds time to spend.

I know my uncle loves me...

because he treats me like his
best friend.

I know my cousins love me...

when we always jump and play.

I know my Pepper loves me...

when she shows me in her very own way.

24

I know Allah loves me..

because He's given me so many
gifts that are definitely not small,

but my wonderful family is by far the best gift of all.

Potato!

Dear Parents,
Thank you for purchasing this book! As a thank you, we've included some suggestions to make this story even more fun, educational, and engaging. The activities below are designed to help your child master different skills such as counting, matching, recognizing shapes, phonics, and more! As you and your child read, you will probably come up with your own fun activities to enjoy and share. Happy reading!
Love,
Randa and Maz

COUNTING

Return to Zaydo Potato's living room and ask your child to count the following:
-Pepper's paw prints
-Zaydo's hand prints
-Rays of sunshine

MATCHING

Pepper made Zaydo Potato's room very messy! Can you help me pair the socks together?

ANIMALS

How many different animals can you find in the book?

SHAPES

Return to the page with the iPads. Can you find the following shapes hidden in these pages?
-heart
-circle
-oval
-rectangle

SPATIAL RELATIONS

Where are Pepper and the potato hidden in every page? Ask your child to use words, such as
-over
-under
-behind
-next to

PHONICS

Zaydo Potato loves his family! Do you know how to spell the word F-A-M-I-L-Y?
Zaydo does!
Find words or objects in the book that begin with the letters
F-A-M-I-L-Y.

Did you enjoy this story?

We hope you did! Check out *Zaydo Potato: Can Allah See Me Now?* for more Zaydo Potato fun! Salams!

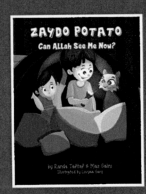

Rummana Publishing Inc
ƐᴅᴜᴄᴀᴛƐ·ƐᴍᴘᴏᴡƐʀ·IɴꜱᴘɪʀƐ

Rummana Publishing is dedicated to educate and provide quality Arabic as a foreign language resources, empower young Muslims with collections of children's books with Muslim characters, and inspire more (but not limited to) Arab and Muslim writers to write and spread love and understanding.

For more fun material visit us at www.rummanapublishing.com

About the Authors:

RANDA TAFTAF
Founder of Rummana Publishing
Randa is a bilingual, Syrian-American born in Youngstown, Ohio.
She grew up in Pennsylvania and moved to Damascus, Syria at the
age of 14. She now lives in Florida with her husband and son Zayd.

Equipped with a fiery passion for languages and an MEd in Foreign
Language Education, Randa is a seasoned foreign language instructor
of 17 years and counting. Over the course of her career, she has managed
and led exemplary ESL programs, actively trained ESL instructors,
developed a curriculum for the teaching of Arabic as a Second Language
and much more. As an American of Syrian heritage, she strives to bridge
the cultures of the east and west through education and storytelling
both inside and outside her classrooms and even in her own home.
Consequently, she founded Rummana Publishing Inc with her husband
Maz to educate, empower and inspire.
Follow her work on Instagram 📷 and Twitter 🐦 @rummanapublishing

MAZ GALINI
Co-Founder of Rummana Publishing
Maz is a Lebanese-American polyglot. Fluent in four languages:
English, Arabic, French, and Spanish, Maz can step inside the mind
and context of other cultures easily. Maz prefers to connect cultures
and express himself more creatively through his work as a web
designer/developer in additon to his writing and exceptional
photography. Sharing in the vision to educate, empower and inspire
his son Zayd and future generations, Maz co-founded Rummana
Publishing Inc with his wife, Randa.
Follow Maz's work on Instagram 📷 @mazgalini and check out
his page www.mazgalini.com

87683920R00022

Made in the USA
San Bernardino, CA
06 September 2018